Usher

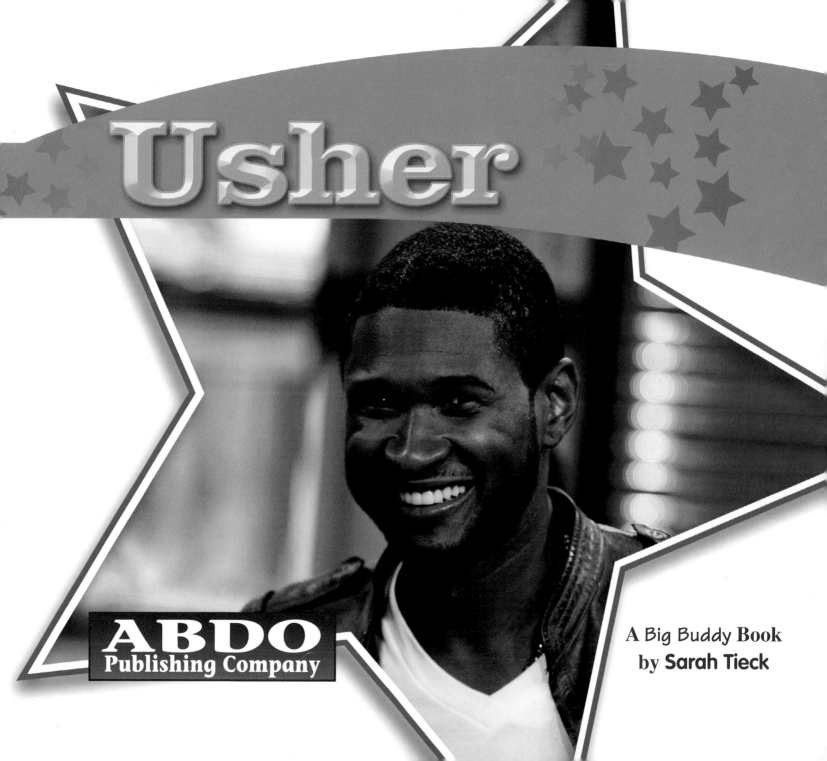

ABDO
Publishing Company

A Big Buddy Book
by **Sarah Tieck**

Published by ABDO Publishing Company, 8000 West 78th Street, Edina, Minnesota 55439.

Printed in the United States.

Coordinating Series Editor: Rochelle Baltzer
Contributing Editor: Marcia Zappa
Graphic Design: Maria Hosley
Cover Photograph: *AP Photo*: Jason DeCrow
Interior Photographs/Illustrations: *AP Photo*: Chris Carlson (p. 12), Jeff Christensen (p. 29), Kevork Djansezian (p. 15), Paul Drinkwater/NBCU Photo Bank via AP Images (p. 11), Ric Feld (p. 9), Bill Haber (p. 27), Peter Kramer (p. 4), Jerome T. Nakagawa (p. 15), Pablo Martinez Monsivais (p. 7), Chris Pizzello (pp. 16, 17), Gus Ruelas (p. 16), Amy Sancetta (p. 25), Matt Sayles (p. 23), John Smock (p. 29), Susan Sterner (p. 9), Mark J. Terrill (pp. 20, 21), Kathy Willens (p. 19); *Getty Images*: Jonathon Wood (p. 12); *Wikipedia.com* (p. 23).

Library of Congress Cataloging-in-Publication Data

Tieck, Sarah, 1976-
  Usher / Sarah Tieck.
     p. cm. -- (Big buddy biographies)
  ISBN 978-1-60453-551-8
  1. Usher--Juvenile literature. 2. Rhythm and blues musicians--United States--Biography--Juvenile literature. 3. Singers--United States--Biography--Juvenile literature. I. Title.

  ML3930.U84T43 2009
  782.421643092--dc22
  [B]
                        2008033924

Usher

Contents

Singing Star 5

Family Ties 6

Growing Up 8

Early Years 10

A New Talent 14

Albums and Awards 18

On Broadway 22

Off the Stage 24

Buzz 28

Snapshot 30

Important Words 31

Web Sites 31

Index 32

Usher sings rhythm and blues music.
This popular music features a strong beat.
It is inspired by jazz, gospel, and blues.

Singing Star

Usher is a talented singer and actor. He has made award-winning albums. And, he has acted in television shows and movies.

Usher's music has made him famous. He has appeared on magazine covers. And, he has been **interviewed** on popular television shows.

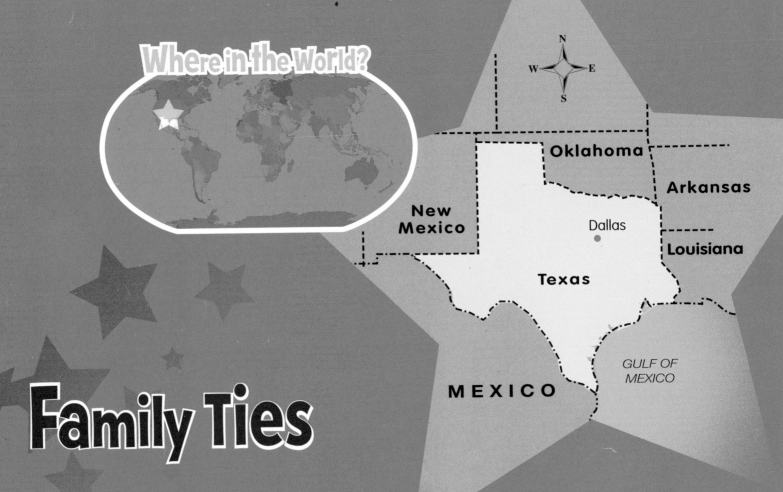

Family Ties

Usher Raymond IV was born in Dallas, Texas, on October 14, 1978. His parents are Jonetta Patton and Usher Raymond III. He has one younger brother named James Lackey.

Usher is known for tumbling onstage.
His grandma taught him to do flips.

Kentucky

Virginia

Tennessee
· Chattanooga

North
Carolina

Atlanta
☆

South
Carolina

Mississippi

Georgia

Alabama

N
W   E
S

Florida

ATLANTIC
OCEAN

GULF OF
MEXICO

Growing Up

Usher's family lived in Chattanooga, Tennessee. When Usher was very young, his parents parted. Usher stayed with his mother.

Usher began singing in a church choir as a young child. When Jonetta realized her son's talent, the family moved to Atlanta, Georgia. They hoped Usher could sing on the talent **competition** show *Star Search*.

Jonetta worked in an office and directed the church choir. Later, she helped Usher with his music.

Usher attended Haynes Bridge Middle School and North Springs High School. These are both near Atlanta.

Early Years

In 1991, Usher got the opportunity he had hoped for. He sang "End of the Road" by Boyz II Men on *Star Search*. He won best teen male **vocalist**!

In Atlanta, Usher sang in many talent shows. He met a lot of people who worked in music. Some of them wanted to help him make an album.

Usher is a talented dancer. Dancing is part of his job, but it is also one of his hobbies.

"Think of You" was a hit song on Usher's first album.

Sean "Diddy" Combs has also been known as Puff Daddy and P. Diddy. He is a well-known rapper, actor, and businessman.

12

When Usher was 15, he went to New York City, New York. There, he worked with Sean "Diddy" Combs to make an album. In 1994, Usher released his first album, *Usher*.

In 1997, Usher released his second album, *My Way*. *My Way* was very popular. For a time, the album had the fourth-highest sales in the United States.

A New Talent

In 1997, Usher also began acting. His first **role** was on a funny television show called *Moesha*. He also got a role on *The Bold and the Beautiful*. He discovered that he loved acting as much as singing!

On *Moesha*, Usher worked with famous singer and actress Brandy. He played her boyfriend on the show.

In 1998, Usher made his **debut** in movies. His first **role** was in a scary movie called *The Faculty*. In 1999, he appeared in *She's All That*. Later that year, he had a starring role in *Light It Up*.

In *Light It Up*, Usher worked with well-known actresses Vanessa Williams (*left*) and Rosario Dawson (*above*).

Usher attends many events. Sometimes fans ask for his autograph or picture.

Albums and Awards

In 2001, Usher **released** another album. It was called *8701*. Usher received Grammy Awards for his work on *8701*. "U Remind Me" won an award in 2001. And in 2002, "U Don't Have to Call" won another.

Each year, more than 100 Grammy Awards are given to the best accomplishments in music. It is a big honor to receive an award.

In 2004, Usher and Alicia Keys sang a duet called "My Boo." They won a Grammy Award for it!

Did you know...

Some people use the word "boo" to mean boyfriend or girlfriend.

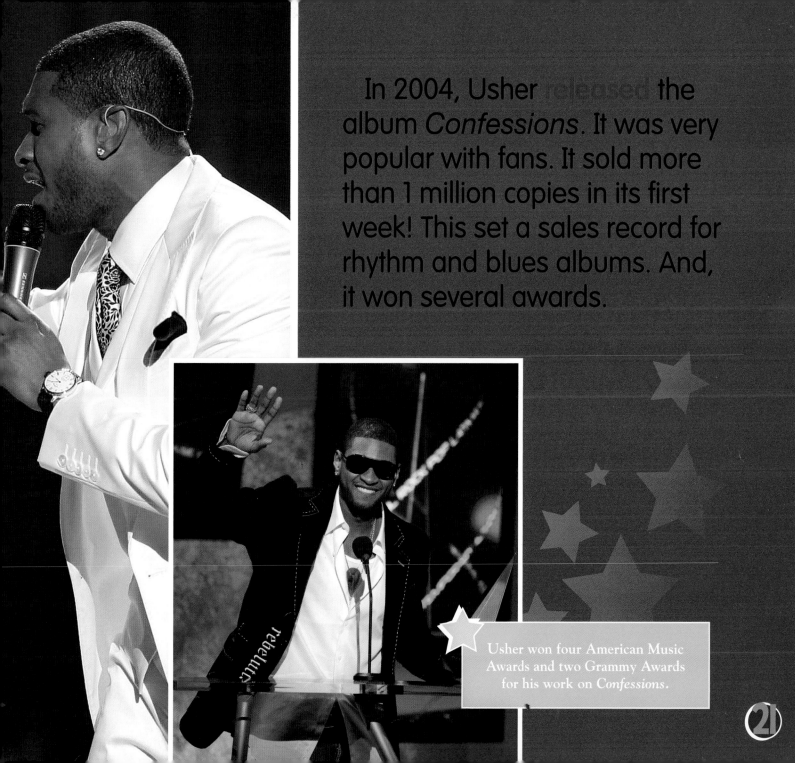

In 2004, Usher released the album *Confessions*. It was very popular with fans. It sold more than 1 million copies in its first week! This set a sales record for rhythm and blues albums. And, it won several awards.

Usher won four American Music Awards and two Grammy Awards for his work on *Confessions*.

On Broadway

In 2006, Usher performed in the **musical** *Chicago*. *Chicago* is a famous, award-winning Broadway show. These theater shows are considered to be some of the best in the country.

Usher performed in *Chicago* for two months. He played a lawyer named Billy Flynn.

In 2007, Usher showed off his theater skills. He performed "Singin' in the Rain" for *Movies Rock: A Celebration of Music in Film.*

Broadway shows are based in New York City. They take place in more than 39 theaters in Manhattan. Many people see a Broadway show while visiting the city.

Off the Stage

Usher is a husband and a father. He married Tameka Foster on August 3, 2007. They soon had a son named Usher Raymond V. Usher, Tameka, and their son live in Atlanta. Usher and Tameka were expecting another child in 2009.

Usher and Tameka often watch Cleveland Cavaliers basketball games. Usher is one of the team's owners.

Usher's New Look set up programs to help victims of Hurricane Katrina. After the hurricane, Usher went to New Orleans, Louisiana, to help clean up.

Usher enjoys helping people. In 2005, he started a **charity** called Usher's New Look.

Each year, Usher's New Look has a camp for teenagers. At Camp New Look, teens learn about working in music and sports. Usher's charity also helps kids get money for school and find jobs.

Buzz

Usher's opportunities continue to grow. In 2008, he **released** the album *Here I Stand*. The songs are about his new life as a husband and a father.

Fans are excited to see what's next for Usher. Many believe he has a bright **future** in music and acting.

Snapshot

★**Name**: Usher Raymond IV

★**Birthday**: October 14, 1978

★**Birthplace**: Dallas, Texas

★**Albums**: *Usher, My Way, 8701, Confessions, Here I Stand*

★**Appearances**: *Moesha, The Bold and the Beautiful, The Faculty, She's All That, Light It Up, Chicago*

Important Words

charity a type of group or fund established to help people in need.

competition a contest between two or more persons or groups.

debut (DAY-byoo) a first appearance.

future (FYOO-chuhr) a time that has not yet occurred.

interview to ask someone a series of questions.

musical a story told with music.

release to make available to the public.

role a part an actor plays in a show.

vocalist singer.

Web Sites

To learn more about Usher, visit ABDO Publishing Company online. Web sites about Usher are featured on our Book Links page. These links are routinely monitored and updated to provide the most current information available.

www.abdopublishing.com

Index

awards **5, 18, 20, 21**

Bold and the Beautiful, The (television show) **14, 30**

Boyz II Men **10**

Brandy **15**

Chicago (musical) **22, 30**

Cleveland Cavaliers **25**

Combs, Sean "Diddy" **12, 13**

Confessions (album) **21, 30**

Dawson, Rosario **16**

education **9**

8701 (album) **18, 30**

Faculty, The (movie) **16, 30**

Foster, Tameka **24, 25, 28**

Georgia **8, 9, 10, 24**

Here I Stand (album) **28, 30**

Keys, Alicia **20**

Lackey, James **6, 8, 10**

Light It Up (movie) **16, 30**

Louisiana **26**

Moesha (television show) **14, 15, 30**

Movies Rock: A Celebration of Music in Film (television show) **23**

My Way (album) **13, 30**

New York **13, 23**

Patton, Jonetta **6, 8, 9, 28**

Raymond, Usher, III **6, 8**

Raymond, Usher, V **24**

She's All That (movie) **16, 30**

Star Search (television show) **8, 10**

Tennessee **8**

Texas **6, 30**

Usher (album) **12, 13, 30**

Usher's New Look **26**

Williams, Vanessa **16**